故園畫憶

庚寅中秋
韓磐陀題

《故园画忆系列》编委会

名誉主任：韩启德

主　　任：邵　鸿

委　　员：（按姓氏笔画为序）

万　捷	王秋桂	方李莉	叶培贵
刘魁立	况　晗	严绍璗	吴为山
范贻光	范　芳	孟　白	邵　鸿
岳庆平	郑培凯	唐晓峰	曹兵武

故园画忆系列
Memory of the Old Home in Sketches

峁梁上的风景
——陇东素记
Loess Hills' Landscape in Eastern Gansu

张学忠　绘画 撰文
Sketches & Notes by Zhang Xuezhong

学苑出版社
Academy Press

图书在版编目（CIP）数据

峁梁上的风景：陇东素记 / 张学忠撰文、绘画. —北京：学苑出版社，2015.9
（故园画忆系列）
ISBN 978-7-5077-4856-7

Ⅰ. ①峁… Ⅱ. ①张… Ⅲ. ①钢笔画—作品集—中国—现代 ②甘肃省—概况 Ⅳ. ①J224 ②K924.2

中国版本图书馆CIP数据核字（2015）第212840号

出 版 人：	孟 白
责任编辑：	周 鼎
出版发行：	学苑出版社
社　　址：	北京市丰台区南方庄2号院1号楼
邮政编码：	100079
网　　址：	www.book001.com
电子信箱：	xueyuanpress@163.com
销售电话：	010-67601101（营销部）、67603091（总编室）
经　　销：	全国新华书店
印 刷 厂：	北京信彩瑞禾印刷厂
开本尺寸：	889×1194 1/24
印　　张：	4.5
字　　数：	100千字
图　　幅：	91幅
版　　次：	2015年9月北京第1版
印　　次：	2015年9月北京第1次印刷
定　　价：	38.00元

目 录

序（一）　　　　　　　　杜大恺
序（二）　　　　　　　　田卫戈
前言

大美庆阳

东老爷山	3
古城罗川赵氏石坊	4
华池双塔	5
罗川古城	6
白马乡	7
北石窟寺	8
塔儿湾石造像塔	9
周祖陵	10
南佐遗址	11
碾盘山	12
黄帝冢	13
南梁革命纪念馆	14
东湖公园一角	15
陕甘边苏维埃政府旧址	16
古石刻艺术博物馆	17
山城堡战役遗址	18
河连湾陕甘宁省政府遗址	19
陇东民俗博物馆	20
环县红军长征纪念馆	21
宁县乡村	22
镇原太平镇小景	23
新兴园	24
午后的打麦场	25
庆阳窑洞民居	26
太白镇街头一角	27
子午岭	28
潜夫山秀色	29
寂静的村庄	30
翟池	31
山居	32
白马池	33
西峰小崆峒山	34
秦道遗韵	35
董志塬	36
夏家沟森林公园	37
陇东皮影戏	38
陇东道情	39
庆阳香包	40
喜宴上的吹鼓手	41
过事情	42
新媳妇	43
荷花舞	44
陇东社火	45

做刺绣的婆姨	46	静宁文庙	72
正宁永和镇	47	静宁清真寺	73
宁县九龙桃花会	48	雾锁崆峒	74
推牌九	49	雷声峰	75
农忙时节	50	五龙山	76
碾场	51	太统山森林公园	77
		米家沟生态园	78

问道平凉

		十万沟——大阴山景区	79
平凉宝塔	55	上晌	80
龙隐寺	56	万宝川农场	81
歇马殿	57	庄浪梯田	82
南石窟寺	58	播种	83
龙泉寺	59	打麦	84
大云寺	60	劳动者	85
石拱寺	61	晒暖暖	86
古灵台	62	午后	87
云崖寺	63	喜上眉梢	88
红崖寺	64	静宁乡党	89
王母宫山	65	合线线	90
成纪古城	66	乐在其中	91
皇甫谧墓	67	归	92
牛僧孺墓	68	锦屏镇集市	93
柳湖公园	69	母与子	94
界石铺红军长征纪念馆	70	小学生	95
泾川温泉	71	上良中学的学生娃	96

Contents

Foreword (1)　　　　Du Dakai
Foreword (2)　　　　Tian Weige
Prolgue

The Beauty of Qingyang

East Laoye Mountain	3
Memorial Archways for Mr. Zhao's Mother in the Old Town of Luochuan	4
Twin Pagoda in Huachi	5
The Old Town of Luochuan	6
Baima Township (literally, "White Horse Township")	7
Beishiku Temple	8
Stone Statue Pagoda in Ta'er Bay	9
Tomb for the Founding Father of Zhou Dynasty	10
Relics in Nanzuo Village	11
Nianpan Hill (literally, "Grinding Base Hill")	12
Yellow Emperor's Tomb	13
Nanliang Revolution Memorial	14
A Glimpse of East Lake Park	15
Former Site of Soviet Government of Shaanxi-Gansu-Ningxia Border Region	16
Art Museum for Ancient Sculpture	17
The Reliecs of Shanchengbu Campaign	18
Relic of Soviet Provincial Government of Shaanxi-Gansu-Ningxia Border Region	19
Folk Culture Museum of Longdong Region	20
Huanxian County Memorial for the Long March of the Red Army	21
Rural Area in Ningxian County	22
A Glimpse of Taiping Town of Zhenyuan County	23
Xinxing Park	24
Wheat Threshing Ground in an Afternoon	25
Cave Dwellings in Qingyang	26
A Glimpse of Street on Taibai Town	27
Meridian Ridge	28
Beautiful Sceneries in Qianfu Mountain	29
Silent Villages	30
Zhai's Pond	31
Mountain Dwellers	32
White Horse Pond	33
Minor Kongtong Mountain in Xifeng	34
The Remains of Highways in Qin Dynasty	35
Dongzhi Plateau	36
Xiajiagou Forest Park	37
Shadow Puppet Show in Longdong Region	38
Folk Art Daoqing	39
Sachet in Qingyang	40
Trumpeter in Wedding	41
Undergoing Things	42

The Bride	43
Lotus Dancing	44
Community Fire Dancing in Longdong Region	45
Ladies Working on Embroidery	46
Yonghe Town of Zhengning County	47
Gathering for Peach Blossoms at Jiulong of Ningxian County	48
Pai Gow, A Domino/Card Game	49
Busy Days in Farms	50
Grain Threshing Ground	51

Quest for Spiritual Pursuit in Pingliang

Pingliang Pagoda	55
Longyin Temple	56
Xiema Hall (literally, "Horse Resting Hall")	57
Nanshiku Temple (literally, "South Cave Temple")	58
Longquan Temple (literally, "Dragon Spring Temple")	59
Dayun Temple	60
Shigong Temple (literally, "Stone Arch Temple")	61
Ancient Lingtai (literally, "Spiritual Platform")	62
Yunya Temple	63
Hongya Temple	64
The Mountain of Heaven Queen's Palace (Wangmugong Mountain)	65
Old Town of Chengji	66
The Statue of Huangfu Mi	67
The Tomb of Niu Sengru	68
Liuhu Park	69
Jieshipu Town Memorial for the Long March of the Red Army	70
Jingchuan Hot Spring	71
Jingning Confucius Temple	72
Jingning Mosque	73
Fog Clouding Kongtong Mountain	74
Thunder Ridge	75
Wulong Mountain	76
Taitong Mountain Forest Park	77
Mijiagou Ecological Park	78
Scenic Spot of Shiwangou Ravine: Dayin Mountain	79
Shangzhi	80
Wanbaochuan Farm	81
Terrace in Zhuanglang County	82
Seeding	83
Wheat Threshing	84
Laborer	85
Basking	86
Afternoon	87
Happy to the Eyebrow	88
Townsman of Jingning County	89
Chatting	90
Enjoy!	91
Return	92
Market in Jinping County	93
Mom and Son	94
Students of Primary School	95
Pupils at Shangliang Middle School	96

序（一）

陇东我没去过，从学忠的画里看到的是如信天游般的坦荡、悠然，风情无限。

近30年中国社会的变化很遽烈，西北地区同样处于这一变化之中，变化的速律比东南沿海地区可能慢一些，但变化的深刻性或比东南沿海地区更甚。在这一变化的过程中，一些曾经的存在可能成为记忆，一些陌生的的东西则陡然成为现实。这一过程中所发生的一切都会形成巨大的心理落差，没有一个人可以对这些变化熟视无睹，艺术家尤其敏感，他们不可能身处这一变化之中而无动于衷。如何用艺术的方式将这一变化记录下来，我相信是许多艺术家愿意面对的，而事实上已有许多艺术家付诸行动，学忠的这部作品就是这种行为的结果之一。

学忠是西北人，在敦煌长大，求学期间曾在外闯荡多年，如今仍在西北工作。他对于中国30年的变化的感受是刻骨铭心的，他用素记的方式把其变化中的所见所闻记录下来，除却作为一个学人对这些变化的思考以外，则更有身在其中的特殊体悟。他做这种选择似乎很自然，不做这种选择反而有些意外。我希望学忠能够坚持下去，若干年后，那些所谓素记则会变得非同寻常，成为活生生的历史印记。

杜大恺

清华大学美术学院教授，博士生导师，中国国家画院公共艺术院执行院长

2014年11月10日

序（二） 水墨陇东的营造

　　陇东与陕北相邻，是黄土高原的一部分。这里有着深厚的文化积淀和悠久的历史，山山水水之间，散发着古老而充满活力的气息。张学忠以水墨画的方式，淡淡描绘出这片土地的文化遗脉和现代生活，呈现出黄土山乡特有的风貌，或许，这是第一次以水墨绘画的形式集中展现陇东文化地标和农村风光的艺术探索，对每一位曾在那里生活的人来说更是一种视觉中的美好记忆。

　　张学忠的水墨以传统的媒介入手，但表现手法却体现出现代人的眼光。摄影角度的呈现和速写式的线墨元素，形成画面强烈的构成形式感，类似于一种视觉意味的"营造"，这使得我们要从另一个角度观赏陇东，即古老沉厚的黄土地与现代生活相融合的角度，亦或是今天黄土高原风貌特征的一种必然的呈现方式。

　　这些水墨作品更是如同一种游牧，让视觉片段的碎片重新组合为完整的图像记忆，陇东，也因这些作品成为一种艺术营造下的不断展现与延伸。

田卫戈
西北师范大学美术学院教授，敦煌学院院长
2014 年 11 月 10 日

Foreword (1)

This collection depicts sceneries in the eastern part of Gansu Province in China, also known as the Longdong Region. The region mainly consists of two cities: Qingyang and Pingliang in Gansu Province.

I have not yet been to the region. However, by enjoying Zhang Xuezhong's paintings of the area, I can discover the candid, relaxed and charming features of Gansu Province, all of which resemble Xintianyou, a folk music style from Shaanxi province, literally means rambling in the sky.

Great changes have taken place in Chinese society over the past thirty years. During the past three decades, some things have disappeared from our lives and have begun to fade into memory, while other things that we never imagined could be possible before have become our new reality. All these fluctuations have left a hole in our collective heart. No one can turn a blind eye to these changes. Artists, in particular, are very sensitive to them. Painters prefer there to be a record of the transition which is created by artistic expression. The collection by Xuezhong is a perfect example of this.

Zhang Xuezhong, a local of northwestern China, grew up in Dunhuang City of Gansu Province. He lived in many different places when he was a student. Today, he has returned to his roots for work. He has felt for himself the great changes that have taken place in this area over the years. He chooses to record the transitions which he has observed and heard through his paintings. As a prominent figure in the art circle, he has his own view regarding the transformation. Moreover, as a witness to the changes, he can feel it even deeper than anyone else. It is my hope that Xuezhong can persevere with his artistic pursuit. After some years, he will be deemed as an extraordinary person who will surely leave his mark on history.

Du Dakai
Professor, PhD Supervisor, Academy of Art & Design, Tsinghua University
Executive President, Public Art Institute, China National Academy of Painting
Nov. 10th, 2014

Foreword (2) Longdong Region in the Eyes of a Painter

Longdong Region, as a part of the Loess Hill Plateau, borders Shaanxi Province. It has a rich cultural heritage and long history. Zhang Xuezhong adopted Chinese brush drawing to depict the unique sceneries of the hilly towns in the Loess Plateau with his gentle style. Perhaps it is the first artistic attempt to use Chinese brush drawing to bring to the audience the cultural landmarks and countryside scenes of Longdong Region. For anyone who has lived there, it evokes a beautiful visual memory.

Zhang Xuezhong's Chinese brush drawing uses traditional tools (Chinese brush). However, his personal artistic style perfectly embodies the preferences of a modern artist. These paintings employ a photographer's perspective and use sketch-like styles with various Chinese ink lines in place. Therefore, the picture has a tremendous visual impact in terms of its layout. Namely, the painter generates a unique visual atmosphere. All these efforts provide us with a different angle to enjoy the scenes of the Longdong region. Depicted in his scenes is a combination of the rich and traditional local features with life in the modern age. It could be said that his way of painting is an essential way to express the characteristics of the region.

These Chinese brush paintings are like nomadism, which recomposes pieces of visual elements into a complete graphic memory. Longdong Region has, as a result, been demonstrated and extended by this artistic creation.

Tian Weige
Professor, College of Fine Arts, Northwest Normal University
President, College of Dunhuang, Northwest Normal University
Nov. 10th, 2014

前　言

　　中国北方梁峁交错的深壑大塬，是由黄土积淀起来的独特景观，苍茫宏阔，生机勃勃，她不仅是地球上最广阔、最深厚的黄土高原，也孕育和塑造了古老的中华文明。

　　位于黄土高原中心腹地的陇东，指陇山（即今六盘山）以东的甘肃地区，包括庆阳、平凉和天水东部部分地区，处于陕、甘、宁三省（区）交汇处。考古发掘的大量史前文明遗存，证明陇东地区是中华文明最重要的诞生地之一。从距今亿万年前的环江翼龙、黄河古象的发现，距今1.8万年前的旧石器石核（我国发现的第一件旧石器）和距今4000多年前南佐遗址的发掘（炎黄民族农耕文明的开始），到2000多年来中国历史重大转折事件的遗迹、宗教信仰的寺观庙宇古迹、形态各异的窑洞建筑，还有千百年传承不灭的香包、皮影、剪纸等不灭的风物习俗，无一不在诉说着陇东这片土地的辉煌与传奇。

　　历经漫长文明史的演变和流转，相较于今天中国东部、南方富庶繁荣的现代文明，陇东地区虽然显得贫瘠落后，但这里保留的众多历史遗迹和人文遗存以及长盛不衰的众多非物质文化遗产，在某种程度上可以看做是可供中国人怀古追远、思省圆真的一个宁静致远的精神家园。由此，学苑出版社"故园画忆系列"的策划者可谓慧眼独到，当然也给了自己一个机会，得以借助画笔审视这个既熟悉又陌生的故园。

　　所谓陌生，是指看惯了高大上、红光亮和酷炫卡的现代绘画图式，面对满眼沟壑黄土的村落、隔世尘封的古迹和朴拙勤劳仍在黄土里刨生活的农民，自己不免心生惶惑，因为偶尔会发现自己写生时猎奇搜旧的假日心态，全然无法与土地及其山川草树和农人相溶；其次是绘画如何能描绘眼前的图景，清新俊逸的布局经营、浪漫奇巧的点染皴擦，无疑是对黄土大塬雄阔厚重品格的误读，秃笔草草、写意抽象，又恐敷衍了生动鲜活的具体情态。

Prologue

The Loess Hills in northern China are visually unique in that they are a result of accumulated sand. These Loess Hills not only constitute the largest and thickest loess plateau in the world, but have also nurtured and incubated the ancient Chinese civilization.

Longdong Region is one of several important "cradles" of Chinese civilization. From the pterosaur fossil discovered in Huanjiang River, which dates back hundreds of millions of years, to the discovery of a stegodon fossil in the former river way of Huanghe River; from the relics that record the transformation of China over two millenniums, to the religious sites which have been in existence for hundreds of years; from cave dwellings with various shapes and forms, to time-honored cultural traditions like sachet making, shadow puppetry, and paper-cutting: all of these are indications of the legendary past of this region.

With the transformation of civilization, Longdong Region is comparatively less developed than the eastern part of China. Nonetheless, the historical sites and cultural relics which are preserved here, in conjunction with various enduring and intangible cultural legacies, can, to some extent, serve as the perfect cultural hub for reminiscing about history and realizing self-improvement.

Today, let's revisit our old home with the Chinese brush. Sometimes, it is familiar to us; while, in other cases, it is not. I am familiar with this region because I spent my life working and living here. Whenever I was out in the field to paint still-life, the objects of my paintings would primarily be of scenes in eastern Gansu Province. Therefore, I have firsthand experience of closely observing the transformations in Longdong's culture and customs.

I am not familiar with this region because I am accustomed to modern ways of painting. When I pick up my brush before the rugged Loess Plateau, I feel alienated as a result of my perplexity. Therefore, I am very cautious in choosing the layout of the painting. How to ensure perfect artistic expression is a difficult decision to make.

Perhaps the attitude we are supposed to have and the method we must adopt is to depict the region with all sincerity and abolish all old-fashioned mentalities. To this end, this collection of paintings endeavors with innovation. Your comments will be highly appreciated.

大美庆阳
The Beauty of Qingyang

东老爷山

又称兴隆山，位于环县东北部，在陕西、甘肃、宁夏交界处，自古有"鸡鸣听三省"的美誉。它还是闻名遐迩的道教名山，道教宫观与自然风光和谐相衬，浑然天成，是观光、旅游的绝好胜地。

East Laoye Mountain

The mountain is located in Huanxian County, which borders Shaanxi Province, Gansu Province, and the Ningxia Hui Autonomous Region. The mountain is a well-known range and a Daoist site. The mountain boasts natural sceneries and exquisite Daoist buildings, making the mountain a wonderful choice for sightseeing and tourism.

| 古城罗川赵氏石坊 |

位于正宁县罗川乡，修建于明万历四十五年（1617年），是明吏部稽勋司郎中赵邦清为其母所建。石坊为三开间，高10米，石料雕凿、镶砌而成。上有浮雕彩绘，有山水、人物、花鸟、庭舍等，画面形象生动，造型逼真。

Memorial Archways for Mr. Zhao's Mother in the Old Town of Luochuan

The archways are located at Luochuan Township of Zhengning County. Built in 1617, the archways have three gateways. The building is as tall as 10 meters and is made of inlaid stone sculptures. There are embossments with colorful paintings on it. The pictures on the archways are vivid and true to life.

华池双塔

原名石塔院，位于华池县，始建于北宋年间，后来经过多次修葺，保留至今。该塔造型秀丽，结构严谨，雕凿细腻，是古代汉族劳动人民智慧和艺术的结晶，具有很高的历史、艺术价值。

Twin Pagoda in Huachi

It is located in Huachi County. Formerly known as Stone Tower Yard, it was built during the Northern Song Dynasty (960-1127). Exquisitely shaped, the twin pagoda has a carefully designed structure and refined style of sculpture. It embodies the wisdom and artistic achievement of the Han people in ancient China with substantial historical and artistic value.

罗川古城

位于正宁县永和镇北部的四郎河边,建于明万历四十五年(1617年)。古城遗迹尚存,被"琴山、泰山、药王山、北华山"四山合围,沃土平畴,阡陌纵横,风景优美。

The Old Town of Luochuan

The old town is located on the north bank of the Silang River in Yonghe Town of Zhengning County. Built in 1617, the relics of the old town can still be found today. The old town is surrounded by four mountains: Qinshan Mountain (Mountain of Musical Instrument), Taishan Mountain, Yaowang Mountain (Mountain of the King of Medicine), and Beihua Mountain. The town boasts fertile and flat lands with much farmland and beautiful scenery.

白马乡

位于华池县西北部，境内梁峁相间，沟壑纵横，属丘陵沟壑农牧区。因境内白马石造像塔而知名，塔越建于北宋年间，六角形，顶残，现存七层，以红砂岩石料凿磨镶砌而成。

Baima Township (literally, "White Horse Township")

It is located in the northwestern part of Huachi County. There are many ridges and loess hills with many ravines. The township is well-known for the White Horse Pagoda. The pagoda was built during the Northern Song Dynasty (960-1127). The layout of the pagoda is hexagonal. The top part of the pagoda was damaged. Currently, the pagoda still has seven floors in existence. It was constructed by bonding polished red sandstones.

北石窟寺

位于庆阳市西南 25 千米处，蒲河和茹河交汇之东岸的覆锤山下。现存大小窟龛 307 个，石雕造像 2126 尊，甘肃省四大石窟之一。

Beishiku Temple

It is located 25 kilometers southwest of Qingyang. There are a total of 307 grottos of different sizes and 2,126 statutes in the temple area. It is one of the top four grottos in Gansu Province.

塔儿湾石造像塔

位于合水县太白乡塔儿湾村,始建于宋代。以凿磨的红砂岩石条块叠砌而成,平面呈八角形密檐式建筑,共13层。

Stone Statue Pagoda in Ta'er Bay

It is located at Ta'er Bay Village in Taibai Township. Built in the Song Dynasty (960-1279), the tower was constructed by bonding boulder strips of polished red sandstones. The layout of the pagoda is an octagon with multiple eaves. The pagoda has 13 floors.

周祖陵

位于庆城县城东山，因山顶有周先祖不窋陵面得名。山顶是以周祖大殿、周王殿等组成的周祖文化景区，布局严谨规范，座落有致。周祖陵历史悠久，钟灵翰秀，自古为游览胜地。

Tomb for the Founding Father of Zhou Dynasty

The tomb is located on Dongshan Mountain in Qingcheng County. It got its name from the tomb at the peak of Dongshan Mountain. The tomb was built for Buzhu, the founding father of the Zhou Dynasty (1046-256 BC). Atop the mountain, there is a cultural scenic spot which consists of the Grand Hall, the hall for the emperor of the Zhou Dynasty. The tomb enjoys a long history and a graceful atmosphere. It has been a site of attraction for tourists since ancient China.

南佐遗址

位于官寨乡南佐村,是新石器时代的遗址。出土的炭化粮食(稻、粟、稷等),是我国古代农业考古的重要材料。据史料记载,这里还是先周农耕文化发源地。

Relics in Nanzuo Village

It is located in Nanzuo Village of Houguanzhai Township. The history of the site can be traced back to the Neolithic Age. It was recorded in history that it was the birthplace of farming culture in the early Zhou Dynasty (1046-256 BC). Carbonized food was unearthed here, which serves as an important archaeological discovery of farming practices in ancient China.

碾盘山

位于子午岭腹地西坡乡，山形如一座大碾盘。相传中国神话人物八仙中的张果老的墓地就在碾盘山下，《庆阳府志》《正宁县志》都有记载："张果老墓在县（罗川）东七十里"，"县东有洞，相传果老隐居炼丹处，故有墓在焉。"但张果老墓地既没有墓碑，又没有铭文，也没有具体位置。故人们称为果老幻墓。这里山风呼呼、芳草萋萋，透过浓云迷雾，或许正是幻墓之名的由来。

Nianpan Hill (literally, "Grinding Base Hill")

It is located in the heart of Ziwu Ridge (literally Meridian Ridge). The mountain is just like a large grinding base. It is said Zhang Guolao, one of the eight legendary immortal Daoist figures, was buried underneath the mountain. However, there is no tombstone, epitaph or exact location for the tomb. This is why the tomb is referred to as "Ghost Tomb of Zhang Guolao".

黄帝冢

位于正宁县境内，椭圆形，面积约 1500 平方米，坐落在五顷原和二顷原之间。《史记·五帝本纪第一》《正宁县志》都有关于黄帝冢记载，它在此，守望着华夏大地，庇佑华夏子孙。

Yellow Emperor's Tomb

It is located in Zhengning County. Oval shaped, the tomb covers approximately 1,500 square meters with two of its sides facing valleys. Yellow Emperor is regarded as the ancestor of the entire Chinese nation. His tomb stays here as if the emperor is watching the land and protecting his descendents.

南梁革命纪念馆

位于华池县南梁乡，馆区牌坊正中刻着胡耀邦题写的"南梁革命纪念馆"。牌坊后面是南梁革命烈士纪念塔，碑座东西两壁及背面刻着刘志丹、谢子长、王泰吉等608位烈士的英名。

Nanliang Revolution Memorial

It is located in Nanliang Township of Huachi County. On the archway of the memorial, the inscription reads, "Nanliang Revolution Memorial." After crossing the archway, there is a memorial tower dedicated to those who gave their lives in the revolution of Nanliang. The names of 608 martyrs are inscribed on the tower.

东湖公园一角

位于庆阳市西峰区九龙路北段，占地约170亩。内有峰、湖、亭、桥观赏景点等游乐设施，园内绿树成荫，环境优雅，是广大游客和市民的游览、休憩场所。图为公园一角的石桥和游船。

A Glimpse of East Lake Park

The park is located in the northern part of Jiulong Road, Xifeng District of Qingyang City. It covers 170 mu (1 mu = 666.67 square meters) and has an elegant atmosphere. The area offers tourists a full range of recreational activities. It is an ideal resort for both tourists and locals. The picture shows the stone bridge and sight-seeing boat on one corner of the park.

| 陕甘边苏维埃政府旧址 |

　　位于华池县林镇乡四合台村的寨子湾，1934～1935年陕甘边区苏维埃政府在此地办公，具有重要的红色教育意义。

Former Site of Soviet Government of Shaanxi-Gansu-Ningxia Border Region

It is located at Zhaiziwan, Sihetai Village, Linzhen Township of Huachi County. It was the office building for the Soviet Government of Shaanxi-Gansu-Ningxia border region. Its relevance to China's revolution highlights its significance.

古石刻艺术博物馆

位于合水县北区，馆舍为仿明清古建风格，占地约3.2万平方米。馆藏文物3000多件，以单体圆雕石造像最具特色，甘肃省第一座以古石刻艺术展览为主题的专题博物馆。

Art Museum for Ancient Sculpture

It is located in northern Heshui District, Qingyang City. It is the only museum in Gansu Province that exhibits ancient sculptures. The hall imitates the building styles of the Ming Dynasty (1368-1644) and Qing Dynasty (1644-1911) and covers 31, 968 square meters.

> 山城堡战役遗址

　　位于环县山城乡以北及大西沟西南、断马崾岘以南地带。1936年，中国工农红军在这里进行了著名的山城堡战役。

The Reliecs of Shanchengbu Campaign

It is located in Shancheng Township of Huanxian County. In 1936, the Chinese Workers and Peasants' Red Army launched the well-known Shanchengbu Campaign to break the siege of Kuomintang. It was a battle of major significance to China's revolutionary history.

河连湾陕甘宁省政府遗址

位于环县洪德乡河连湾村,是 1936 年 7 月~1937 年 9 月中共陕甘宁省委、省苏维埃政府所在地。现为甘肃省国防教育基地。

Relic of Soviet Provincial Government of Shaanxi-Gansu-Ningxia Border Region

It is located in Helianwan Village, Hongde Township of Huanxian County. From July 1936 to September 1937, it was the site for the CPC Party Committee Office and the Soviet Provincial Government Office of Shaanxi-Gansu-Ningxia Border Region.

陇东民俗博物馆

位于庆阳市南郊小崆峒农耕民俗文化村内,始建于 1986 年。馆藏历史文物 1058 件,民俗精品 1200 多件,农耕器具 200 多件,具有浓郁的民俗特色。

Folk Culture Museum of Longdong Region

It is located in the village for showcasing farming culture in minor Kongtong in the southern suburb of Qingyang City. Built in 1986, the museum is home to many types of historical relics, folk culture exhibits, and farming equipment displays. All of these features bring a sense of authenticity to the museum.

环县红军长征纪念馆

位于环县，建于 2007 年。由三件间土箍窑构成，展品为民间征集来的革命文物 30 多件。毛泽东、彭德怀等领导人长征途中曾在此居住。

Huanxian County Memorial for the Long March of the Red Army

It is located in Huanxian County, Qingyang City of Gansu Province. Built in 2007, the memorial consists of three sand-made cave dwellings. The exhibits, which are collected from the public, consist of over 30 pieces of cultural relics from the revolutionary age

宁县乡村

宁县窑洞有 5000 多年的历史渊源。近年来随着农村经济的发展，农民生活的提高，多数人已弃窑盖房，但仍有一部分人居住在窑洞中，这种新旧民居混杂一处，成了宁县乡村一特点。

Rural Area in Ningxian County

The cave dwelling in Ningxian County can be traced back over 5,000 years. However, with the development of the rural economy, many people have abandoned this type of residence. This is why a combination of both old and new dwellings can be found in this area.

镇原太平镇小景

位于镇原县，名优特产有杏子、黄花、烤烟、苹果等，也是当地著名的书画之乡。图为小镇街道匆忙的行人。

A Glimpse of Taiping Town of Zhenyuan County
The town is located in Zhenyuan County. Its local specialties include: apricot, daily lily, flue-cured tobacco, and apples. The town is also famous for its calligraphers and painters. The painting shows busy pedestrians on the streets of this town.

新兴园

位于西峰后官寨乡沟畎村，是集休闲度假、风情旅游、餐饮住宿于一体的大型自然生态园区，建有窑洞宾馆、高尔夫球场、保龄球馆、网球场等设施。

Xinxing Park

It is located in Gouquan Village, Houguanzhai Township of Xifeng District. It is a large, natural ecological zone which incorporates vacation opportunities, resorts, folklore tourism, and catering.

> 午后的打麦场

夏忙季节天气很关键，不光要抢收，还要抢在阴雨天气来临之前晾晒和打场。午后的打麦场上空无一人，只有艳阳下晾晒的小麦。

Wheat Threshing Ground in an Afternoon

The weather during the peak days of summer farming is critical. While harvesting as fast as possible, farmers have to thresh wheat and dry it in the sun. In the afternoon, it is too hot to thresh the grain. Thus, the only thing to observe during this time is the wheat drying under the beautiful sunshine.

庆阳窑洞民居

窑洞历史悠久，先周时期人们就根据当地自然地理条件不同人们就地取材，建有不同形式的窑洞，主要有依崖而建的"崖庄"和以塬面为基础而建的"地坑庄"。这种传统黄土窑洞的居住形式，是庆阳民俗发展项目的重要内容。

Cave Dwellings in Qingyang

Cave dwellings have a long history. Different types of cave dwellings were built in accordance with the local natural and geographic conditions. There are two types of such dwellings: one is built on cliffs, while the other type is constructed on a plateau in Loess Hill. This traditional form of residence is an important element in Qingyang's attempt to develop folklore tourism.

太白镇街头一角

位于合水县，镇区山清水秀林木茂盛，有"小江南"之称，是秦汉以来要塞之一，以旧时建有"太白金星"庙而得名。近年来，太白镇依靠推广水稻种植技术治理盐碱地，出产的太白大米口味醇香，成为闻名陇上的粮中珍品。

A Glimpse of Street on Taibai Town

The town is located in Heshui County. The town has charming sceneries with dense forests. This is why the town is referred to as a place that "resembles the humid southeast part of China". The town got its name from the Taibai Temple built in ancient China. The town produces Taibai rice, a local specialty in Longdong Region.

> 子午岭

　　子午岭地跨陕西、甘肃两省，处于黄土高原的腹地，因与本初子午线方向一致，故称子午岭。庆阳子午岭林区是黄土高原目前保存较好的一块天然植被区，也是保存完整的天然水源涵养林区。

Meridian Ridge

The ridge crosses Gansu Province and Shaanxi Province. It is located in the heart of the Loess Plateau. The ridge obtained its name because it runs parallel to the meridian line. The forest area in Meridian Ridge is a relatively complete area on the Loess Plateau which has natural vegetation and forest for conserving water.

潜夫山秀色

位于镇原县城北,因柏林密布,古柏参天,又被称为柏山。潜夫山因东汉末年著名思想家、政治家、哲学家王符(85~162年)隐居于此并著有《潜夫论》一书而得名。

Beautiful Sceneries in Qianfu Mountain

The mountain is located in the northern suburb of county town of Zhenyuan County. The mountain got its name after the well-known book, A Paper in Qianfu was written by Wang Fu, a celebrated thinker, statesman, and philosopher in the late period of the East Han Dynasty (25-220). The mountain is also referred to as Cypress Mountain because of the dense forest of tall cypress trees on its hills.

寂静的村庄

庆阳地区的沟沟卯卯之间，散布着众多古村落，寂静而厚重。人文始祖轩辕黄帝在庆阳曾与中医鼻祖岐伯论医，有《黄帝内经》行世，庆阳因此也被称为"岐黄故里"。

Silent Villages

Qingyang has a long history and profound cultural heritage. In these valleys and plateaus, there are many ancient villages that remain today – silent and stately.

翟池

位于庆阳镇原县东 35 千米，崀肖公路西侧的上肖境内。因此地聚居翟姓，故曰翟池。池上游南端有泉注入池中，水质甘甜纯净，是当地人畜饮用的重要泉池，也是人们夏季避暑休闲度假之地。

Zhai's Pond

It is located in Zhenyuan County. The pond was named after the extended family of the Zhai family, who made their home here. There is a spring that pours into the pond. The water here is sweet and clear. In addition, it is an ideal vacation resort in the summer.

> 山居

庆阳地区林业资源丰富，全市现有林业用地面积约 2072 万亩，占国土总面积 51%。在山区林场茂密的树丛中，一幢小屋里的住户可能是守望绿色的护林员，亦或是离开黄土尘世的隐居者。

Mountain Dwellers

There is a large forest in Qingyang City. In the thick forest, there are some cottages. These scattered dwellings are home to forest rangers and the solitary.

亦称白马泉,在庆阳镇原县东,因为当地有白马庙,故称白马池。

White Horse Pond

It is located to the east of Zhenyuan County and Tunzi Town. It is also referred to as White Horse Spring. It obtained its name from a local temple called White Horse Temple.

西峰小崆峒山

位于庆阳市西峰区董志乡，因与平凉崆峒山有"姊妹山"之谓而得名。山势呈凤凰卧巢状，山上有座无量祖师殿，因此又称凤凰山、无量山。

Minor Kongtong Mountain in Xifeng

It is located in Xifeng District in Qingyang City. The mountain got its name "Minor Kongtong Mountain" because it is referred to as the sister mountain of Kongtong Mountain in Pingliang City. The appearance of the mountain is like a crouched phoenix. There is a hall for Master Wuliang (also known as Emperor Zhenwu). For these reasons, the mountain is also called Phoenix Mountain and Wuliang Mountain.

秦道遗韵

约公元前212年，秦国在雄奇险峻的子午岭之上建成了中国古代唯一沿山脊和高地选线的国家级交通大道，称为秦道或秦直道。庆阳子午岭秦道线形顺直，弯道很大，道路标准被誉为中国高速公路之祖。

The Remains of Highways in Qin Dynasty

The highways of the Qin Dynasty (221-206 BC) were built in 212 BC. They are the only major transportation routes built on the ridges and highlands in ancient China. These roads feature direct routes, gentle curves, and standardized construction. For these reasons, the roads are referred to as the forefathers of modern Chinese highways.

董志塬

位于泾河北岸、马莲河和蒲河两大河流之间,是庆阳市第一大塬,也是黄土高原最大的一块塬面,号称天下黄土第一塬。这里历史渊源,名胜古迹灿若星辰,原野风光引人入胜。

Dongzhi Plateau

The plateau is located on the north bank of Jinghe River and is situated between the two streams: Malian River and Puhe River. It is known for being the largest plateau on China's Loess Hills and is also the largest plateau of its kind in the world. Various historical sites and cultural relics are scattered around the Dongzhi Plateau. Its wild scenery is particularly appealing.

夏家沟森林公园

位于合水县，子午岭森林覆盖面积完整、原始的地段，公园各类设施完善。

Xiajiagou Forest Park

It is located in Heshui County. The park is situated in the area where the forest density is the thickest in Ziwuling Forest (literally Meridian Ridge Forrest) and the natural conditions are intact. The park has all types of facilities and is the first choice for tourists.

陇东皮影戏

陇东地区古老的民间艺术，是秦陇文化与周边族群文化相融合、古老的道情与皮影相结合的产物，相传产生于宋代。民间俗称"灯影戏"、"小戏"、"老道情"。在千百年的发展演变中，集中华皮影之大成，撷当地道情曲艺之精华，成为当地人民倾诉情感、丰富文化生活综合性艺术。

Shadow Puppet Show in Longdong Region

It is said that the play originated from folk art during the Song Dynasty (960-1279). After hundreds of years of transformation, the local play was able to learn from the advantages of similar shows in China and incorporate the essence of the local Daoqing opera into its own style. It is a comprehensive artistic form for local people.

陇东道情

　　源于甘肃庆阳、环县一带,由民间艺人赶着毛驴,驮着锣鼓乐器,用皮影艺术表演。以一人说唱,众人帮唱,说唱相间,以唱为主的传统艺术形式表现。陇东道情产生的具体年代,现已无法考察。

Folk Art Daoqing

This type of folk art originated in Huanxian County and Qingyang City of Gansu Province. Folk artists would put musical instruments, like the gong and drum, on donkeys and tour around for performances. When performing Daoqing, artists would sing the opera during the shadow puppet show. One singer would take the lead to talk and sing while others would sing the chorus with him or her. Daoqing, as a traditional art, combined the artistic form of talking and singing and emphasized the latter.

庆阳香包

香包又称荷包、香囊、佩帏、容臭，庆阳俗称"绌绌"或"耍货"，端午节制作和佩带"绌绌"是当地的一种习俗。庆阳香包的起始时间已经无法考证，但现存的古老的"千岁香包"制作于是宋代，距今至少有800多年的历史，庆阳也被誉为"香包刺绣之乡"。

Sachet in Qingyang

The embroidery of sachets, also known as "small bags", is popular among local folks. Qingyang is widely known as the hometown for sachet making. The earliest sachet in existence today is the "Millennium Sachet" from the Song Dynasty (960-1279).

喜宴上的吹鼓手

庆阳地区许多农村至今仍保留婚庆喜宴上聘请吹鼓手助兴的习俗，往往都是村里多才多艺的能人担当吹鼓手。吹鼓手根据红白喜事不同的需要、不同仪式和过程，演奏出各种各样的调子，悲哀的、喜庆的，什么场合吹什么曲，吹出人生的喜怒哀乐。

Trumpeter in Wedding

During weddings in rural areas, trumpeters who masters many types of music would be invited to play. These trumpeters were skilled in playing tunes for a variety of ceremonies and customs that expressed the full range of emotions one has in life.

过事情

陇东人的婚丧大事俗称"过事情",过事情的习俗中表现出庆阳地区人们浓厚的家庭、家族观念。图中婚礼上是妆扮一番长辈等待新人的叩拜。

Undergoing Things

"Undergoing things" is a term used by local folks in Longdong to indicate the hosting of weddings and funerals. The various customs demonstrated during these process show the strong loyalty of Qingyang people to the nuclear family and extended family. The painting shows the senior family members dressed-up and waiting to be greeted by the bride and groom, who are kneeling in respect.

新媳妇

　　庆阳地区有天快黑时迎娶被涂丑的新媳妇的传统，待新娘到新郎家妆扮一新与新郎举行庆祝仪式。图中新人们正在举行寓意快乐过日子的礼仪。

The Bride

In Qingyang, people usually paint the face of the new bride before night time to make her appear ugly as the wedding ceremony is about to begin. This is a local custom. Later, the bride will visit the home of the groom and redo her make-up for the celebration. The painting shows the couple is celebrating the ritual, which symbolizes the happiness they hope to bring into their new life together.

荷花舞

庆阳西峰区是周先祖公刘开创中国农耕文化的起源地，并孕育出民间荷花舞，对周文化在民间的遗传具有一定的研究价值，是世界非物质文化遗产的组成部分，并载入《20世纪中国民族舞蹈经典》，庆阳也因此被中国民俗学会命名为"荷花舞之乡"。

Lotus Dancing

This type of dancing originated from the remaining customs of the Zhou Dynasty (1046-256 BC) and the nurturing of farming culture. It is one of the world's many intangible cultural heritages. This is why Qingyang was named by the China Folklore Society as the "Hometown of Lotus Dancing."

陇东社火

以社为单位"击器而歌,围火而舞",故称社火。人们载歌载舞,高亢激越的配器和浓郁的乡土气息,更加显示了当地人们淳朴憨厚、豪爽剽悍的性格。

Community Fire Dancing in Longdong Region

This type of dancing is community-based. People would sing accompanied by percussion instruments and dance around the fire. That is why it got the name "Community Fire Dancing". The joyful dancing and singing in conjunction with the dynamic background music and rich cultural atmosphere during the performance highlight the frankness, modesty, straightforwardness, and agility of local people.

> 做刺绣的婆姨

刺绣是庆阳地区民间艺术中的一大类，其分布面广，以庆阳、正宁两县的刺绣最为有名。刺绣艺术源远流长，有着深厚的群众基础，而其独特的风格在老少传承、新旧更替中愈发焕发出迷人的光彩。图是婆姨们正在讨论刺绣。

Ladies Working on Embroidery
Embroidery in Qingyang has a long history and was widely practiced by local people. Its unique style has been passed down from one generation to the next and is currently being updated. All these factors bring a certain glamour to the art. The painting shows ladies discussing embroidery.

> 正宁永和镇

位于正宁县西南部,有正宁"南大门"和"苹果之乡"的美誉。商贸活动活跃,起到强大的辐射带动作用。

Yonghe Town of Zhengning County

It is located in the southwestern part of Zhengning County. It enjoys a reputation as the southern gateway of Zhengning County and the "town of apples". With its vibrant commercial activities, the town exerts a powerful influence over the economic growth of the region.

宁县九龙桃花会

　　位于宁县城以东的九龙川河谷地带，是宁县名产黄甘桃产地。每年阳春三月桃花盛开，争奇斗艳的桃花香飘数百里，当地人们和外来游客都会从四面八方赶来游春、赏花、喝茶。

Gathering for Peach Blossoms at Jiulong of Ningxian County

It is located in the valley of Jiulongchuan area. It is the "home of the Golden Sweet Peach", a kind of peach unique to Ningxian County. Every spring, when the peaches blossom, the effect is like a large festival of flowers. This time is referred to as the "Gathering for Peach Blossoms". The place is ideal for taking in the sights of spring and admiring the beautiful flowers.

| 推牌九 |

民间流传较广的一种游戏，包括骨牌和纸牌两种形式，是当地人娱乐消遣一种方式。

Pai Gow, A Domino/Card Game
The game is very popular among the locals. It consists of two forms: one with Chinese dominoes and one played as a card game. It is a means of entertainment for many people here.

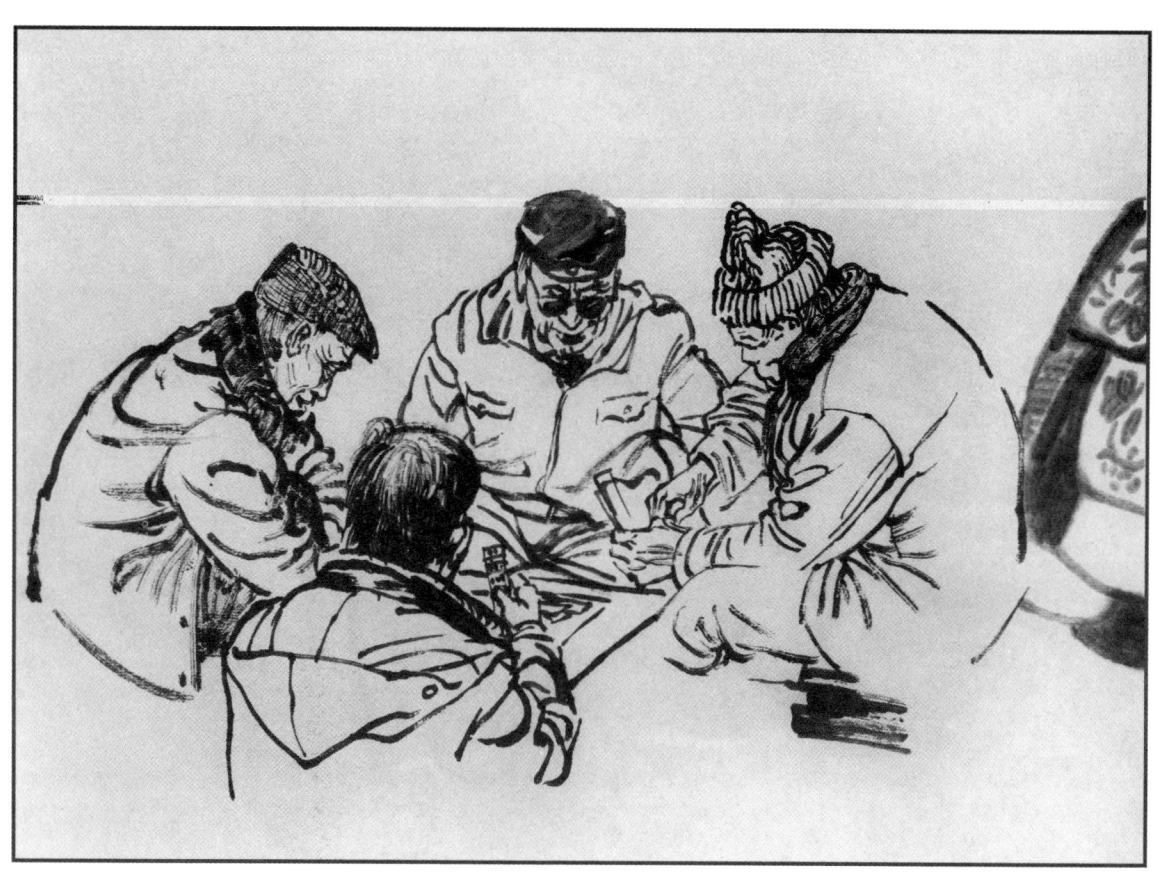

> 农忙时节

　　农家读书的孩子，不仅要功课好光耀门庭，也要在农忙时节回家务农成为田间好手，否则会被村里人看不起。

Busy Days in Farms
As farmers' children, they are supposed to be good farm-hands. Otherwise, they will be looked down upon by villagers.

> 碾场

又称打场，农民小麦收割后，用拖拉机拖带石质或铁质碾子环绕麦场一圈圈碾压，周围人们不断翻起碾压麦草反复碾压，致使小麦脱壳。

Grain Threshing Ground

The area for threshing grain is also known as the mashing ground. After wheat is harvested, tractors will be employed to drag a stone or iron threshing roller to grind the ground many times. While doing so, people keep the wheat on the bottom aloft so as to remove its shell.

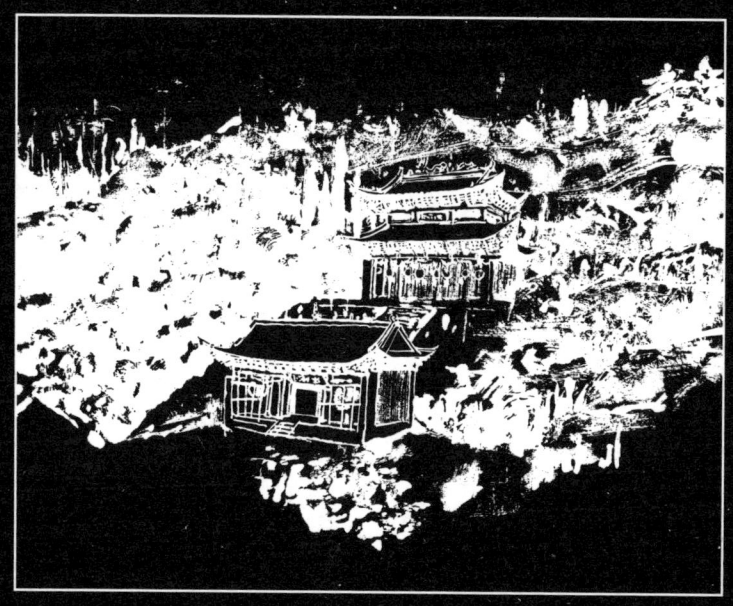

问道平凉
Quest for Spiritual Pursuit in Pingliang

平凉宝塔

建于明代，砖塔，八角七层，高约31米，塔雕造工艺精湛，整体粗壮宏伟。平凉宝塔所在地原为佛寺，有长方形城墙护卫一周，东有明代修建的东岳庙，西有明代修建的真武庙和紫金城。

Pingliang Pagoda

Built during the Ming Dynasty (1368-1644), the pagoda is made of bricks with an octagonal layout and seven floors. It is about 31 meters tall. The sculpture on the tower is exquisite. The tower has a robust and magnificent exterior. To the eastern side of the pagoda is the Temple of God of Mount Tai. To the western side of the pagoda is the "temple for Taoist legendary Emperor Zhenwu" and Heavenly Purple City.

龙隐寺

　　位于平凉市区，建于汉唐时期，初名兴教寺，是皇帝降旨命名。龙隐寺建在悬崖上，山的中下部有四眼泉，寒暑不变其形，旱涝不改其盈。

Longyin Temple

It is located in Pingliang City. Built in the Han Dynasty (202 BC-220 AD), it is also referred to as Xingjiao Temple (literally, "prospering Buddhist Temple"). The temple was built on a cliff. On the middle and lower parts of the mountain, there are four wells, which offer water regardless of changes in season and weather.

歇马殿

位于平凉市,主要有歇马殿山门、圣母殿、观音堂等佛教建筑群。曾记载,公元 65 年明帝派人赴天竺迎佛取经,路上阴雨连绵无法前行,在此驻足一月余,期间译经传教,后来人们把住过的店坊改为佛殿,起名"歇马殿"。

Xiema Hall (literally, "Horse Resting Hall")

It is located in Pingliang City. The hall has a set of Buddhist buildings, such as the gateway, Goddess Hall, and Avalokitesvara Hall. The hall was also recorded in history: in 65AD, Emperor Ming of the Han Dynasty (202 BC-220 AD) sent envoys to India to obtain Buddhist classics. During the journey, it had been raining so heavily that the delegation had to stop for one month here. During their stay, they translated Buddhist classics and preached. After that, the place where they stayed was renovated into a hall for Buddhist purposes and was renamed as Xiema Hall (literally, "Horse Resting Hall").

南石窟寺

位于平凉市泾川县,现存 5 窟,1 号东大窟和 2 号西小窟保存较为完整。其中,东大窟为南石窟寺的主窟,高达 13 米,宽约 17 米,深 14 米,结构独特,造型宏伟。

Nanshiku Temple (literally, "South Cave Temple")

It is located in Jingchuan County, Pingliang. There are currently five grottos still in existence. In particular, the No.1 east main grotto and No. 2 west minor grotto remain basically intact despite the passage of time. The No.1 east main grotto is the main grotto in the temple. The grotto is as tall as 13 meters, about as wide as 17 meters, and as deep as 14 meters. The grotto is uniquely structured and spectacular to behold.

龙泉寺

　　位于平凉居芮河北岸，由山麓林带、芮谷、东台、中台、西台等几部分组成，其中中台为胜景区，景区面积1.5平方千米。背依风翥山，四季滴水不断，因此闻名。

Longquan Temple (literally, "Dragon Spring Temple")

It is located at the north bank of Ruihe River of Pingliang City. The temple consists of several parts: a forest, Ruigu Valley, East Flatland, Middle Flatland, and West Flatland. Middle Flatland is the most beautiful part and covers 1.5 square kilometers. The temple, with Fengzhu Mountain to its back, has water drops falling all year round. This is why it is referred to as "Dragon Spring Temple."

大云寺

位于泾川县，隋仁寿元年（601年）高僧将14粒舍利于送到泾川，在大兴国寺建地宫，置函，供养。武则天时期大兴国寺发现了隋代供养的舍利，重新瘞葬砖筑地宫，建塔立寺，改称大云寺。改成大云寺。现在其遗址建有大云寺博物馆，为仿唐建筑风格。

Dayun Temple

It is located in Jingchuan County. In 601, eminent Buddhist monks brought 14 pieces of Sarira to Jingchuan. An underground palace was built underneath the Daxingguo Temple with a case to pay tribute to it. During the reign of Empress Wu Zetian (684-705), Daxingguo Temple was renamed Dayunshan Temple. On the former site of Dayunshan Temple, there is now a Dayun Temple Museum built in the Tang Dynasty (618-907) architectural style.

石拱寺

位于华亭县上关乡半川村，开凿于北魏延昌元年（512年）。窟群坐北向南，依崖开窟，窟释分布于东西约120米长的沙质石崖上，现存窟龛14个。

Shigong Temple (literally, "Stone Arch Temple")

It is located in Huating County. Built in 512, the temple has a group of grottos facing south. These grottos were carved into the cliffs. The length of the grottos is about 120 meters from east to west. 14 grottos remain intact today.

古灵台

位于平凉市灵台县城内,始建于公元前11世纪商纣时期,是周文王征服了位于今灵台县百里镇一带的密须国后,为祭天昭德、与民同乐所筑。

Ancient Lingtai (literally, "Spiritual Platform")

It is located in Lingtai County of Pingliang City. The platform was constructed during the 11th Century BC, during the reign of Emperor Zhou of the Shang Dynasty (1600-1046 BC). It was built by King Wen of the Zhou Dynasty. King Wen took the lead in overturning the Shang Dynasty (1600-1046 BC) and built the platform to honor heaven, highlight virtues, and celebrate with his fellow citizens.

云崖寺

位于平凉庄浪县距县关山自然森林峡谷深处，始凿于北魏后期，明朝时进入鼎盛时期，从清末开始逐渐衰落。在以云崖寺为中心，方圆不到 5000 米的范围内，有著名的八大寺以及店湾、店峡、木匠爷崖石窟和三教洞，形成一条蔚为壮观的石窟群。

Yunya Temple

It is located in Pingliang City, Zhuangliang County. The temple was built in the late Northern Wei Dynasty (386-534). Less than 5 kilometers from the temple are the well-known Eight Temples Grotto, Dianwan Bay Grotto, Dianxia Gorge Grotto, grotto on the cliff in memory of the carpenter master, and the Three Religions Grotto (The three religions refer to Buddhism, Daoism and Confucianism). All of these constitute a spectacular group of grottos.

红崖寺

位于庄浪县，北魏至明朝时期建造的大型石窟群，至今已有 1600 多年的历史。

Hongya Temple

It is located in Zhuanglang County. The temple has a large group of caves built from the Northern Wei Dynasty (386-534) to the Ming Dynasty (1368-1644). The temple has a history of over 1,600 years.

| 王母宫山 |

　　位于在泾川县，泾、芮二河交汇的三角地带，传为周穆王与西王母欢宴于山阳瑶池，临行时爱不忍舍，一再回头观望，由此得名，并在汉武帝元封年间，在山上修建了王母宫。

The Mountain of Heaven Queen's Palace (Wangmugong Mountain)

The mountain is in the triangular zone in Jingchuan County where the Jinghe River and Ruihe River converge. It was built in the Yuanfeng Period (110-104 BC) during Emperor Wu of the Han Dynasty's reign (202 BC-220 AD). The mountain received its name because of the legendary romance between Heaven Queen and Emperor Mu of the Zhou Dynasty (1046-256 BC).

| 成纪古城 |

位于静宁县治平乡刘河村,为西汉所置成纪县治。城址总面积 25 万平方米,城址为正方形,今存约 14 万平方米,西北部和东部残留城墙长 490 米。整个故城址压在新石器时代文化的遗址上,具有一定的历史价值。图为古城城墙遗址一角。

Old Town of Chengji

Located in Liuhe Village, Zhiping Township of Jingning County, the old town covered 250, 000 square meters and was square-shaped. Currently, the site is as large as 140, 000 square meters. The remaining walls in the northwestern and eastern parts of the city are as long as 490 meters. The entire old town has remained on its original site since the Neolithic Age. The old town has a lot of historical value. The painting shows a part of the remaining part of the town wall.

皇甫谧墓

皇甫谧墓位于甘肃省灵台县。皇甫谧（215～282年）字士安，安定郡朝县（今甘肃省平凉市灵台县朝那镇）人，三国西晋时期学者、医学家、史学家，东汉名将皇甫嵩曾孙。他一生以著述为业，其著作《针灸甲乙经》是中国第一部针灸学的专著。

The Statue of Huangfu Mi

The tomb is located in the graveyard of Mr. Huangfu Mi in Lingtai County. Huangfu Mi, a scholar, doctor, and historian in the Three Kingdom Period (220-228) and the Western Jin Dynasty (265-316), spent his life writing books. His masterpiece, A-B Classic of Acupuncture and Moxibustion, is China's first monograph in the field.

牛僧孺墓

位于灵台县新开乡牛村，牛僧孺为唐代宰相，著名的政治家、文学家，殁后葬于家乡，现存陵墓保存完好。

The Tomb of Niu Sengru

The tomb, located in Niucun Village, Xinkai Township, Lingtai County, is the final resting place of Prime Minister Niu Sengru of the Tang Dynasty (618-907). The Prime Minister was a famous statesman and litterateur. He was buried in his hometown after his death. His tomb is well-preserved today.

柳湖公园

　　位于平凉市城区的中心，地形西高东低，南坡北平，各湖均有潜水泛流，有百泉之说，是陇东著名的自然山水园林。

Liuhu Park

It is located at the center of Pingliang City. The western part of the park is higher than its eastern part. The southern part is sloping and the northern part is flat. The lakes in the park have springs underneath them. This is why the park is said to have 100 springs. The park is a well-known natural resort in Longdong Region.

界石铺红军长征纪念馆

位于平凉市静宁县界石铺镇继红村。这里曾是中国工农红军长征两次途经和三大主力胜利会师的地区之一。毛泽东、周恩来等中央领导曾在这里宿营扎寨，留下了许多珍贵的历史资料。

Jieshipu Town Memorial for the Long March of the Red Army

The memorial is located in Jihong Village, Jieshipu Town, Jingning County of Pingliang City. It is one of regions twice covered during the "Long March of the Red Army." It is also one of the regions where the three main forces of the Red Army joined together. Mao Zedong, Zhou Enlai, and other leaders from the central authority had camped here and left with many valuable materials of historical significance.

泾川温泉

位于泾川县何家坪，开发利用始于于1971年，热水层厚164米，常年恒温38.2℃，泉水含有13种活性微量元素，是当地避暑疗养、休闲度假胜地。

Jingchuan Hot Spring

The hot spring is located in Hejiaping of Jingchuan County. The use of the spring started in 1971. The hot water layer is 164 meters thick. The temperature of the spring maintains a temperature of 38.2℃. With 13 active microelements in the water, the spring has become a popular resort for summer vacations and leisure activities.

静宁文庙

　　静宁文庙建筑群，顺中轴线依次为先师庙门、戟门、大成殿，戟门内为四合院落。整个布局主次分明，造形独特，气势宏伟，是明代具有代表性的建筑。

Jingning Confucius Temple

The layout of the architecture of the Jingning Confucius Temple is symmetric with buildings placed one after another. The layout highlights the main functional buildings. The architecture employs unique shapes to a magnificent effect. It is an architecture characteristic of the unique styles of the Ming Dynasty.

静宁清真寺

　位于静宁县城站院巷内,始建于明嘉靖十四年(1536年),是穆斯林宗教活动的主要场所。现存的礼拜大殿面积390平方米,平面呈"凸"字形,由歇山、悬山顶和两坡卷棚连接,建筑形式独特,古建筑中少见。

Jingning Mosque

The mosque is located in the county town of Jingning, Gansu Province. Built in 1536, the mosque has a long history. The existing main hall is 390 square meters. The layout, when viewed from above, is a T-shaped building. The structure has nine ridges altogether with overhanging gable roofs and two-sided, round, ridged roofs. This unique structure is rarely found on ancient buildings.

雾锁崆峒

　　中国道教发源地的平凉崆峒山，是道教主流全真派的圣地，也是天然的动植物王国。其间峰峦雄峙，危崖耸立，似鬼斧神工，林海浩瀚，烟笼雾锁，如缥缈仙境。

Fog Clouding Kongtong Mountain

It is the cradle of Daoism in China. The mountain is a perfect home for flora and fauna with magnificent ridges and a huge forest. All these transform the mountain into a heavenly place.

> 雷声峰

　　位于平凉崆峒山，是主峰马鬃山向南延伸的一条支脉，宛如主峰的一条右臂，舒展而下，指向涛涛的前峡河水。雷声峰为丹色石质，岩壁陡峭，下临深渊，在雷雨时节雷声在空谷依栏而望，崆峒激荡，犹如山崩地裂，惊人心魄，故取名"雷声峰"。

Thunder Ridge

It is located on Kongtong Mountain of Pingliang. The rock of the ridge is red. Additionally, the ridges are cliff-like. On the lower part of the ridge, there is a deep pond. In rainy seasons, thunder will echo throughout the empty valley, which can be quite frightening. This is why the ridge is referred to as "Thunder Ridge".

五龙山

位于崇信县铜城乡古峡口，位于芮河南岸，属关山东麓之余脉。有"五龙捧圣"之称，昔为西戎咽喉要地。

Wulong Mountain

It is located in Tongcheng Township of Chongxin County. It is on the extended ridge of the eastern part of Guanshan Mountain. Wulong Mountain is referred to as a range with five dragon-like cliffs. It was a military hub against its enemies to the west.

太统山森林公园

位于平凉市崆峒区西郊 3.5 千米处，占地面积 21.7 万亩，省级自然保护区和森林公园，是天然动植物园。

Taitong Mountain Forest Park

It is located in the western suburb of Hongtong District of Pingliang City. The park covers 217,000 mu (1 mu = 666.67 square meters). It is a natural park for flora and fauna, a provincial-level natural conservation area, and a forest park.

米家沟生态园

位于华亭县东峡林场，占地2800多亩，平均海拔1600米，年平均气温7～8℃，森林覆盖率67.6%，植被丰茂，林壑优美，动植物资源丰富，自然景观独特。

Mijiagou Ecological Park

It is located in Dongxia forest station in Huating County. It covers 2,800 mu (1mu = 666.67 square meters). The average altitude of the mountain is 1,600 meters. The park has dense plants, beautiful wooded areas and ravines, and many diverse types of plants and animals.

十万沟——大阴山景区

位于平凉崆峒山西南麻武乡,十万沟——大阴山景区位于平凉崆峒山西南。史书记载,昔日轩辕黄帝登崆峒问道时,曾将十万军马隐于沟内,石崖间"将军窑""藏军洞""击鼓窑"以及"仓房梁""将官墓""仰驾山"等古遗址仍存。

Scenic Spot of Shiwangou Ravine: Dayin Mountain

It is located in Mawu Township, to the southwest of Kongtong Moutain, Pingliang City. It is the area where the Yellow Emperor visited during his hike up Kongtong Mountain for philosophical enlightenment. According to history, he hid his 100,000 soldiers in the valley when visiting the moutain some 5000 years ago. On the cliff, we can find General's Cave Dwelling, Bunker Cave, Drum-hitting Cave, Warehouse Ridge, and Officer's Tomb. All these ancient relics are still in existence today.

上畤

公元前220年秦始皇首次西巡,到达莲花台"上、下畤",祭祀炎黄二帝,开创了祭祀炎黄的先河,成为华夏民族的又一祭祀圣地。

Shangzhi

It is said this place is the location where the first emperor of the Qin Dynasty (221-206 BC) paid tribute to Emperor Yan and the Yellow Emperor, both of whom are deemed as ancestors of the Chinese nation. His ceremony started the tradition of paying tribute to the two emperors, thereby turning this place into a sacred land for Chinese people.

万宝川农场

位于灵台县新集乡，是一个典型的山区农场。全场拥有土地14.7万余亩，生长着豆科牧草和冬花、大黄等30多种野生药材，以及满山遍野杜李、山桃、酸枣、核桃、槭树和桑树等经济林。

Wanbaochuan Farm

It is located in Xinji Township of Lingtai County. It is a typical farm nestled in a hilly area. On the farm, we can find a legume pasture, Tussilago farfara, rheum palmatum L., and many other types of natural medicinal plants. Trees grown for their produce such as plum trees, mountain peach trees, wild jujube, nut trees, maple trees, and mulberries, can be found in every corner of the farm.

庄浪梯田

被誉为"梯田王国",层层梯田如雕如塑,如诗如画。其"山顶沙棘戴帽,山间梯田缠腰,埂坝牧草锁边,沟底穿鞋"的生态梯田综合治理模式,将黄土高原描绘成一幅景色迷人的风景画。

Terrace in Zhuanglang County

The county is referred to as "Kingdom of Terrace" (Chinese translation) because of its various sculpture-like terraced fields and picturesque scenes. This place is indeed a real painting on the Loess Plateau.

> 播种

　　辛勤的农民把种子撒在土地里,也播在心田中,地里的种子刚刚盖上土,心里的期待已经开始萌发。

Seeding

Hard-working farmers not only plant seeds into the soil, they also plant them in their hearts. Once the botanical seeds are planted, the seeds within their hearts for prosperity have already started to flourish.

打麦

夏收时，打麦的工作总算收尾。夕阳中的麦草垛上霞光闪闪，像是给喧闹了一天的麦场催眠，又像是给疲惫农人深情的赞歌。

Wheat Threshing

During the summer harvest, farmers manage to complete all their tasks. The dusk pours its glitter on the stack of wheat. It is just like a lullaby for the farm, which has been busy all day. It is also a paean for the weary farmers.

> 劳动者

平凉的农村大多保留类似合作社的劳作模式，几家合作集中收庄稼，由庄家地的主人家提供午餐。辛苦劳作后田间午餐的人们。简单的午餐，也能吃的津津有味，一个故事一句笑话，化解所有疲劳。

Laborer

The picture shows farmers picnicking after hours of hard work in the morning. A simple breakfast after so much work is satisfying; a story or joke during lunch can relieve weariness.

晒暖暖

　　平凉农村的老人喜欢寻一个向阳的旮旯,边"晒暖暖"边拉家常,村里的怪事、新闻,田间地头的活计,永远也说不完道不尽。

Basking

Rural senior citizens find a place with sunshine and start chatting. This is a means of entertainment and leisure time in the countryside.

> 午后

　　午后的阳光静谧而安详地散在农家院落，尘世的喧哗仿佛都顿停了下来，爷孙俩和身边的黄狗各想各的心事。

Afternoon

It's afternoon in a rural yard and everything seems to have stopped. Grandfather, his grandson, and their yellow dog are all thinking about their individual worries.

喜上眉梢

民间多以喜鹊喻喜庆之事，再借用"梅"与"眉"之同音，平凉剪纸中多有"喜上眉梢"的剪纸作品，寄托百姓对美好生活的向往。

Happy to the Eyebrow

The locals usually think that the magpie represents happiness. And winter-sweet is the homonym of eyebrow. In the paper cutting of Pingliang, artists would typically use the phrase "Happy to the Eyebrow" (with images of magpies and winter-sweet on paper-cutting) to embody the fervent hope of local people for a happy life.

> 静宁乡党

古代500家为党，12500百家为乡，合而称乡党。甘肃陇东地区和陕西一带人们用来对同一地区老乡、同乡人称呼。

Townsman of Jingning County

"Townsman" is the word usually used by people in Longdong Region of Gansu and Shaanxi Province to refer to their fellow villagers.

> 合线线

　　农民的生活离不开斧锄钩耙，也少不了针头线脑，不论男女，都会在闲暇时晒着太阳捻棉绳或麻绳，也叫合线线。

Twisting Threads and Ropes

Threads and ropes are an indispensable part of a farmers' daily tools. Everyone makes cotton thread and hemp ropes while they bask in the sun during their spare time. It is also referred to by locals as "twisting lines".

乐在其中

陇剧起源于汉代的道情说唱，1959年正式命名，是陇东民间广为流传的曲艺形式。农闲时节，左邻右舍乡亲欢乐聚会。

Enjoy!

Long Opera (Note: Long is the transliteration of the opera's Chinese name and the word does not refer to the length of the opera) originated from a form of folk art known as Daoqing during the Han Dynasty (202 BC-220 AD). Long Opera officially obtained its name in 1959 as a popular folk form in Longdong Region. During their spare time, farmers would gather together with their neighbors to perform Long Opera.

| 归 |

　　平凉农村的许多年轻人，为了生计和梦想，往返于家乡与城市之间。返村的年轻人除去鼓鼓的行囊，还有城里的故事。

Return

Many young people in the rural areas of Pingliang traveled from their hometowns to the cities to make a living and realize their dreams. The youngsters return home for the approaching Spring Festival. As they unpack their bags, they take with them their stories of the urban areas.

锦屏镇集市

位于平凉市崇信县，天然的自然条件，加之经济近年来发展较快，因此带动集市的发展，特产小吃和土特产深受人们欢迎。

Market in Jinping County

The market is located in Chongxin County of Pingliang City. The favorable natural conditions and rapid economic development in recent years are increasing the growth of the market. Local cuisines and specialties are particularly welcomed.

> 母与子

　　泾河是平凉的母亲河,昔日每年的端午节,泾河人有到泾河洗手脸、净眼的习俗,大人和小孩可以尽情在水中嬉戏。

Mom and Son

Jinghe River gave birth to Pingliang. During every Dragon Boat Festival in the past, people in the region would come to Jinghe River to wash their hands, faces, and eyes. Adults and kids would play as they made wishes.

> 小学生

天真无邪的童年，有数不清的快乐的理由。跳绳、丢沙包也会发明出无数种玩法。

Students of Primary School

With the innocence of childhood, the kids would develop numerous ways of jumping rope and throwing small earth bags.

> 上良中学的学生娃

　　始建于 1969 年，以"启智、创新、养德、育人"为校训，让我们有理由相信，富有勤苦精神和创新梦想的少年，必将成为陇东乃至整个祖国未来的脊梁。

Pupils at Shangliang Middle School
Built in 1969, the junior high school's motto is "Inspiration, Innovation, Virtue, and Cultivation." These young students, with their diligence and innovative spirit, will surely become the future backbone of Longdong Region and China.